P9-CLE-776

Planning in Plain English

Writing Tips for Urban and Environmental Planners

Planning in Plain English

Writing Tips for Urban and Environmental Planners

Natalie Macris

PLANNERS PRESS
AMERICAN PLANNING ASSOCIATION
Chicago, Illinois
Washington, D.C.

Copyright by the American Planning Association
122 S. Michigan Ave, Suite 1600, Chicago, IL 60603
ISBN (paperback edition): 978-1-884829-40-6
ISBN (hardbound edition): 1-884829-41-4
Library of Congress Catalog Card Number 99-76662

Printed in the United States of America
All rights reserved

Book production and cover design by Charles Eaton

Contents

Part II: Writing Clearly

Foreword

This book is one of the most important books a planning professional can read, and I am delighted that Natalie Macris has written it. You won't learn here about the benefits of transit-oriented development, the merits of new urbanism, or the fiscal impacts of land use planning decisions. What you will learn is in fact more important; you will learn how to communicate planning ideas and concepts clearly and effectively.

Planning is tremendously important work for the communities we live in, for the environment within and surrounding those communities, and for the economies of those communities. Work this important needs to be well-written and understandable, and that is the focus and importance of this book.

What is a lawyer doing advocating plain English, you might ask? After all, hasn't the legal profession given us so much jargon and gobbledygook? Well, there has been something of a quiet revolution in the legal world ever since Richard Wydick published a small volume called *Plain English for Lawyers* (now in a fourth edition from the Carolina Academic Press). One of the areas where it is particularly important for lawyers to communicate clearly is land use and environmental law, a part of legal practice that is commonly far too filled with jargon, acronyms, and expressions mysterious to the lay reader.

The same problems that plague many lawyers plague many planners. Land use plans can easily be filled with jargon, acronyms, and just plain bad writing. When that happens, the citizens who live with the plan are less likely to know what it means. In addition, jargon excludes people, creating an inside group that knows all the catch phrases and a larger outside group that does not. That frustrates public involvement in planning.

The lessons in this book are not particularly complicated, and that might lead a reader to underestimate their importance. That would be a mistake. Good planning depends on good writing, and planners who read this book and take its lessons to heart will do better work as a result.

Michael H. Zischke, Attorney
Chair of the California Environmental Quality Act and Land Use Practice Group
Landels Ripley & Diamond LLP, San Francisco

Acknowledgments

I am very grateful to Mike Zischke for his interest in and help with this project, and to Sylvia Lewis, Director of Publications at the American Planning Association, for her guidance and support.

Eric Macris, Ruthe Macris, Dean Palos, Jane Bassett, Jean C.R. Finney, Tom Haas, Warren Jones, Leslie Katz, and Brian Thompson provided many invaluable ideas and suggestions. Bob Harrison of Robert L. Harrison Transportation Planning supplied the pithy definitions of Level of Service F in the "Explaining Technical Information" chapter.

Special thanks go to my parents, Dean Macris and Marjorie Macris–planners who write well, and whose distinguished careers inspired this book.

Introduction

A well-written plan or other planning document can be a valuable resource for citizens, decision-makers, government agencies, consultants, and many others. It can keep a planning process moving smoothly, advance policies, prevent misunderstandings, head off legal challenge, and even improve the public's perception of government.

Then why are so many planning documents hard to read, understand, and use? There are many reasons. Some planning documents are difficult to write clearly because they need to "please everyone," from citizens who want to know what will happen in their neighborhood to lawyers who may need to defend the planning organization against a lawsuit. Political pressures can make planners "soft-pedal" controversial points, rather than write in clear, direct statements. Esoteric legal requirements have made some planning documents longer and introduced complicated terminology. Meanwhile, schedule and budget constraints mean that most planners do not have much time or money to spend on editing and rewriting, let alone adding maps or other graphics that would make their documents more interesting to read.

This book suggests ways of avoiding the common writing and organizational problems that can make planning documents less effective. Part I ("Getting Started") provides tips for understanding your readers and organizing your document so that it will be easy to understand and use. Part II ("Writing Clearly") focuses on the most common writing foibles of the planning profession.

Each chapter in Part II ends with practice exercises designed to help you recognize and avoid these bad habits. An exercise key follows Part II.

This book concentrates on the writing idiosyncrasies of the planning field. It is not a complete guide to writing and grammar. That said, many of the suggestions in this book are basic rules that you will find in almost any guidebook about writing. The reference list at the end of the book suggests other useful (and in most cases more comprehensive) sources of information and guidance on better writing. Please refer to those sources for a more thorough review, and use this book to sharpen your awareness of the special writing quirks of the planning profession.

Another point to keep in mind: Almost no one follows all of the rules all of the time. Sometimes there are good reasons for this; the possible exceptions noted throughout Part II of this book describe just some of those occasions. It's also possible that you are (or will be) working in an office that has already set up report formats and standard language requirements that violate "the rules" and make clear communication more difficult. You may not have the time (let alone the clout) to make wholesale changes. In these instances, you may just have to do the best you can and recognize that change, like the planning process itself, usually happens one small step at a time. The same applies to your own process of becoming a better writer.

Part

I

Getting Started

Knowing Your Readers

Have you ever noticed that when you are writing a memo or sending an e-mail to a colleague, someone you know well and like, the words flow more easily and naturally than they would if you were writing, say, a report to a City Council? In your note to your colleague, your writing style is more relaxed and informal; you may be less concerned with how your writing "sounds." Perhaps most importantly, you are thinking about your colleague while you are writing. What information does he or she need? How can I convey that information clearly?

When you are writing a document that more than one person will read, it is often more difficult to keep your readers in mind. They may be a very diverse group. They may be the general public–many different people with widely varying education levels, interests, and concerns.

It can be a big challenge to keep that many different people in mind while writing. That's why it's easy to fall into the habit of writing without considering the people who will be reading. Unfortunately, that habit leads to a lot of unclear writing; if you have lost track of your readers, you probably won't be communicating directly with them when you write.

For that reason alone, it's worth thinking about your readers–who they are, what they need–before you start writing. Knowing who your readers are will help set the tone and organization of your document. Here are some questions you might consider.

HOW MANY READERS?

Are you writing to one person? If so, is that person an employer? An employee? Another colleague? A citizen? If you are writing to more than one person, is it a limited audience (a board or commission, for example)? Or are you writing to a much broader readership, such as a planning commission and the general public?

If you are writing to one or a few people whom you know well, a casual, conversational tone may be perfectly appropriate. A more formal tone is often advisable if you are addressing a larger group or people you don't know well.

WHO ARE THEY?

What are your readers like? How old are they? How much education do they have? Are they likely to be familiar with planning issues? What frame of mind might they be in when they read what you are writing? Curious? Annoyed with you or your organization? Upset about the project you are describing? Should you do any research to find out more about your readers before you start writing?

Knowing as much as possible about your readers will help you keep them in mind and communicate directly with them. You will have a better sense of whether they will understand technical terms, and how much you will need to explain.

WHAT INFORMATION DO THEY NEED?

What will your readers be looking for in your report? Technical information? Policy statements? Analysis of what will happen if a project is approved? Your recommendation?

What information is likely to be most important to your readers? Will some readers be looking for one thing, while others need something else? For example, suppose you are a local government planner, and you are writing a report about a proposed housing development. The report is addressed to the Planning Commission, but architects, engineers, and the general public will also be reading it. The Planning Commission will probably be most interested in your recommendation. The project architects and engineers will be looking for technical information (conditions of approval, for example). And the neighbors may be most concerned with your analysis of how the project will affect their property values and traffic in their neighborhood. How can you make sure that everyone finds the information they need?

Considering these questions will help you organize your document and lead readers to the information they are most interested in.

HOW WILL THEY USE YOUR DOCUMENT?

Will your readers read your document from front to back? Or will they scan it quickly to find the information they are most interested in? Will they read the document just once, or keep it as a reference? The answers to these questions will help you set up the document format and decide what information should come first.

Do you want your readers to do something once they have read your document? Take an action? Use the information you provide? Agree with your recommendation? Form opinions of their own? The answers to these questions can guide you in setting both the tone of your writing and the format of your document. For example, if you want your readers to agree with your recommendation and take an action, you may want to set out the recommendation up front, follow it with a persuasively written justification, and sum up by repeating your recommendation.

Once you have considered these questions, you can think about how to organize your document with your readers in mind.

Organizing Your Document

Typically, a planner's most important writing task is to organize large amounts of information in a form that readers can easily understand. Doing that well requires forethought. This chapter suggests some ways to plan and structure your document that you will want to consider before you start writing. Thinking about the questions listed here will help you draft an outline of your document. While doing an outline may seem like a holdover from grade school, it is still a step well worth taking before you start writing. This is especially true if you are starting from scratch, with no predetermined format for your document.

This suggests an important caveat: If you work for an agency that has already set up standard report formats, you may not be able to follow all of the suggestions offered here. Perhaps, though, you can incorporate some of these ideas while still working within the preordained report structure.

WHAT IS THE MAIN MESSAGE?

Knowing the main message that you want to convey is the key to organizing your document. You will usually want to move as quickly as possible to the main message, or highlight it in some way so that your readers can find it easily. For example, if you are writing a report to a planning commission, your main message will probably be your recommendation about the action the commission should take. You may want to make the recommendation early in the report, and then follow it with supporting analysis and technical information.

Planning reports often present a hierarchy of ideas or a series of main points. Thinking about your document in this way can help you to identify the main message or messages, the secondary messages, the order in which to present them, and ways to connect them. Doing this is usually the first step in setting up an outline. Consider the "inverted pyramid" writing model used in journalism. Most news stories describe the most important information–who, what, when, where, why, and, if possible, how–in the first paragraph, with the paragraphs that follow providing progressively less important information. This ensures that the main message comes across at the very beginning. Readers can then scan through the remaining paragraphs and decide how much more they want to know.

WHAT CAN YOU LEAVE OUT?

Planners generally like to provide lots of information. Unfortunately, all of that information sometimes buries the main message of a report. Consider carefully what you can leave out, put in a table or chart, or move to an appendix. This is especially important if you are writing for a very diverse readership. For example, if you are writing a report to a city council summarizing a traffic study, you might consider highlighting the main points in your report and moving the traffic count data to an appendix. That way, traffic engineers and other interested readers can still find the technical information, but your main message to the council ("traffic will be at gridlock at 5:00 PM," for example) won't be lost.

Consider setting page limits to keep your information-providing tendencies under control. This is a useful way to make sure that your document keeps its focus and doesn't overwhelm readers with data.

DOES THE DOCUMENT NEED HEADERS?

Headers can help you to organize your ideas and outline your report. They break up the report into shorter sections, group related ideas, and lead your reader through the document. They can call attention to important points.

Make sure that the headers are easy to understand. Phrasing headers as questions can be one way of catching the reader's eye and communicating the message of each section clearly. For example, when outlining a neighborhood urban design plan, you might use headers like "How tall can new buildings be?" and "How much can be built on any one property?" These are catchier headers than "Height Limitations" and "Floor Area Ratio Requirements."

DOES THE DOCUMENT NEED A SUMMARY?

Providing a summary section is a very useful way of communicating clearly. A summary often allows you to pare down your report to plainer language, highlight the main message, avoid difficult terminology, and break away from cumbersome but legally required report formats. A summary is often especially helpful when you have a diverse group of readers who are all looking for something different in your document. In a report to a planning commission, for example, a summary could highlight your recommendation and other key information that the commission needs to know. The remainder of the report could then provide the technical information that may be less critical to the commission's decision, but that project proponents and neighborhood groups will want to have.

ARE THERE WAYS TO MAKE THE DOCUMENT LIVELIER?

As a final step before you start writing, consider ways of making your document livelier. Here are some possibilities:

Using Personal Pronouns

Consider whether you could use personal pronouns ("you," "we," "us," "our," "ours") in addressing your readers. Personal pronouns make your document clearer and livelier by keeping your sentences shorter and more conversational. Using personal pronouns can be especially appropriate in memos and in lists of instructions. (For example, in an instruction list for design review applications, "You will need to submit a full-size set of plans to the Planning Department" is a friendlier statement than "A full-size set of plans shall be submitted to the Planning Department.") Keep in mind, though, that personal pronouns create a more casual tone that may not be suitable for longer, more formal documents, such as a general plan or environmental impact report.

Keeping Paragraphs Short

Long paragraphs often look like massive, insurmountable blocks of words on a page. Your readers' eyes may skip right over them. Breaking up long paragraphs into shorter ones can make the text easier to read.

Using Graphics

Tables, photographs, and other graphics also break up long blocks of text and add visual relief to your document. They can convey some types of information more clearly and quickly than the written word. Some people grasp visual material more easily than words. (For other people, though, the reverse is true.) To be certain that your message will get across to everyone, don't let graphics speak for themselves; plan to describe each one in writing, too. The best graphics reiterate and build on what's in the text.

Using Highlights and Sidebars

Consider highlighting important phrases, sentences, or paragraphs in bold, italic, or underlined font. Or, set off key ideas in boxes or in sidebars in the margins.

Setting Margins and Line Spacing

Your readers might appreciate wide margins and ample space between lines of text, especially if your document is a draft. This will give them room to edit and take notes.

# # #

You now have an idea of how you will organize what you have to say. The next step is to say it as clearly as you can.

II

Writing Clearly

3❧

Writing Simple
Sentences

Planning inherently involves the future. Yet in truth, no one can be certain about what will happen in the future. This means that as planners we are constantly dealing with uncertainty. We offer thoroughly reasoned opinions and carefully calculated projections, but we know there is a chance that things will not happen the way we say they will. We may even be more aware of uncertainty than most other people are because we know how tenuous the assumptions behind opinions and projections can be.

When you are uncertain about something, it is natural—and usually advisable—to qualify what you say about it. In writing, though, the need to qualify things can breed long, complicated sentences that are hard to understand. Planners write this way all the time. Instead of writing that a project "may" do something, we write that it "may have the potential to" do it. Qualifying things further, we write that the project "may have the potential to" do it "depending on" a long list of factors. Tack on enough qualifiers and a sentence becomes so long that the message is lost. The writer hides behind a statement that the reader cannot easily understand.

When you are uncertain, it is also natural to try to sound smarter than you actually are. Long sentences with lots of fancy words can give the illusion of intelligence. They can conceal the fact that a writer does not have confidence in the message.

You may sometimes be uncertain because you don't completely understand the message yourself. If you haven't mastered your topic, you will probably not be able to write about it clearly. Again, long sentences with complicated words are a tempting, but ultimately not very effective, form of camouflage. Readers often can sense when a writer is bluffing.

Whatever our reasons, when we write overly long, complicated sentences, we neglect our main responsibility as writers, which is to make it easy for readers to understand our work.

WRITING SHORT SENTENCES

As a rule, each sentence you write should:

- be short (no more than 20 to 25 words long), and
- express only one main idea.

Short sentences that deliver one idea at a time are usually easier to understand. They also force you, the writer, to think more carefully about the message of each sentence. Using short sentences can be especially effective when you are explaining a process or a sequence of events.

Examples:

Long Sentences: The 1990 Comprehensive Plan recommended an "urban limit line" that represented the ultimate urban boundary of the City of Shangri-La as envisioned by the Comprehensive Plan. Last year, however, the voters of the city passed a ballot initiative establishing an "urban growth boundary" that differs in some ways from the urban limit line recommended in the Comprehensive Plan, in that it includes an area consisting of 10 acres that is located at the southern end of the city outside the urban limit line.

Shorter Sentences: The 1990 Comprehensive Plan recommended an "urban limit line" as the City of Shangri-La's ultimate boundary. Last year, however, a voter-approved initiative established an "urban growth boundary" that differs from the "urban limit line." The "urban growth boundary" encompasses an area that is outside the "urban limit line." The added area consists of 10 acres located at the southern end of the city.

In the above example, the two long sentences have been divided into four shorter ones, following the "one-idea-per-sentence" rule. Extra words and phrases (like "ballot" and "of the city") have also been removed.

Here's another example:

Long Sentence: When you submit your use permit application, make sure that you include a written description of the use and 10 copies of the project plans, which will be distributed to the Planning Commission for review before the public hearing date scheduled by City staff after your application is received.

Shorter Sentences: Your use permit application should include a written description of the proposed use and 10 copies of the project plans. When you submit your application, City staff will schedule a date for a Planning Commission public hearing. The Planning Commission will receive your project plans before the hearing date.

Possible Exceptions

The short, one-idea sentence is generally a good rule. For variety, however, you might try using some long sentences, too. (For example, the first few paragraphs of this chapter have some long sentences.) Interspersing short and long sentences can keep your writing from becoming dull and choppy. If a sentence is long, be especially careful to use familiar words so that it is easy to understand.

Most of the time, short sentences are refreshingly direct. When explaining a complicated permit process, for example, the clear, direct, short-sentence approach is usually best. Sometimes, though, short sentences are the written equivalent of hitting someone with a blunt instrument. When you are writing about a personnel problem or some other delicate situation, for instance, longer sentences can help soften the blow. Consider this example:

This memo summarizes our evaluation of the City of Atlantis Community Development Department. It focuses on the professional and management capabilities of the Community Development Director. It recommends actions the City might take.

Sounds ominous for the Community Development Director, doesn't it? Here is a rewrite that says close to the same thing, but a little more gently:

This memo responds to your request that we evaluate the City of Atlantis Community Development Department, focusing particularly on the Community Development Director, to determine if there are any problems of professional or management capability and to recommend any actions the City might take.

The rewritten sentence is long (44 words) and expresses roughly five different ideas. It is a slightly less direct statement than the first example. In this case, though, it might be a more appropriate introduction to a potentially delicate subject.

REMOVING EXTRA WORDS

To write a short, simple sentence, you will need to remove any extra words. It sounds easy, and often is. Table 1 lists simple words that are usually good substitutes for the wordy phrases found in many planning documents.

Table 1
REMOVING EXTRA WORDS

Instead of:	*Try:*
adequate number of	enough
as a means of	to
as per (as in "as per our telephone conversation")	as ("as you asked")
as to	about, on
at the present time	now
at the time	when
at this (that) point in time	now, then
because of the fact that	because

by means of	by, with
despite the fact that	although, even though
does not include	lacks, excludes, omits
during such time	while
during the course of	during
excessive number of	too many
for the period of	for
has a requirement for	needs
in accordance with	by, under, following
in addition	also, besides, too
in an effort to	to
in a timely manner	on time, promptly
in case	if
in cases in which	when, where, whenever, wherever
in closer proximity	closer
in lieu of	instead, rather
in light of	because
in many cases	often
in many instances	often
in order that	for, so

in order to	to
in regard to	about, on
in the event that	if
in the interest of	for
in the nature of	like
in the near future	shortly, soon
in the process of	(omit)
in this regard it is of significance that	(omit)
in view of the fact	because
incumbent upon	must
is able to	can
is authorized	may
is empowered	may
is intended to	(omit)
is unable to	cannot
it is interesting to note that	(omit)
it is important to add that	(omit)
it may be recalled that	(omit)
it is probable that	probably
it would appear that	apparently
no later than	before
not able	unable

not often	rarely
not the same	different
not many	few
not...unless	only if
not...except if	only if
not...until	only when
notwithstanding the fact that	although
on the part of	by
owing to the fact that	because
prior to	before
subsequent to	after
the manner in which	how
the question as to whether	whether
to the effect that	that
under the provisions of	under
until such time as	until
with a view to	to
with reference to	for
with regard to	about
with respect to	about

Sources: Plain Language Action Network; Office of Investor Education and Assistance, U.S. Securities and Exchange Commission; National Archives and Records Administration, Office of the Federal Register.

Planners also have some special writing quirks that produce long, wordy sentences. Here are a few:

The "Over-Qualified" Sentence

As noted earlier, planners like to qualify their conclusions. There is nothing wrong with doing that, as long as you don't use so many words that the reader becomes confused.

Examples:

Wordy Sentence: The project could potentially be expected to increase the rate and volume of drainage runoff.
Simpler Sentence: The project may increase the rate and volume of runoff.

In this case, the word "may" easily substitutes for the wordy phrase "could potentially be expected to."

Wordy Sentence: A low-to-moderate potential for trench wall instability exists on this site.
Simpler Sentence: Trench walls on this site may be unstable.

The main message here is that the trench walls "may be unstable." The phrase "low-to-moderate potential for trench wall instability" is a wordy, bureaucratic way of stating this message. The writer of the wordy sentence may be trying to impress readers with his or her "expert" opinion.

The Complicated Land Use Description

Planners often needlessly use words like "activities," "operations," "facilities," and "area" in describing land uses and actions. While these words may make the writing seem more technical, they usually add unnecessary clutter to a sentence.

Examples:

Wordy Sentence: The project will provide a golf course facility.
Simpler Sentence: The project will provide a golf course.

Wordy Sentence: Grading activities will begin in the spring.
or: Grading operations will begin in the spring.
Simpler Sentence: Grading will begin in the spring.

Wordy Sentence: The "Open Space" designation includes marshland areas, bayland corridors, and waterfront recreational facilities.
Simpler Sentence: The Open Space designation includes marshes, bay lands, and waterfront recreation.

The "In Terms Of" Sentence

A sentence that uses the phrase "in terms of" is often an unclear and wordy sentence. You can usually rewrite the sentence to remove this vague phrase.

Examples:

Wordy Sentence: This report reviews the project in terms of its consistency with local and regional plans.
Simpler Sentence: This report reviews the project's consistency with local and regional plans.

Wordy Sentence: In terms of parking, the project does not meet Zoning Ordinance requirements.
Simpler Sentence: The project does not meet the Zoning Ordinance's parking requirements.

The "As To" Sentence

Another commonly used phrase that usually produces a bureaucratic-sounding (and sometimes muddled) sentence is "As to".

Examples:

Wordy Sentence: City staff recommends that the applicant provide more information as to the proposed landscaping.
Simpler Sentence: City staff recommends that the applicant provide more information about the proposed landscaping.

Wordy Sentence: We are unclear as to the Park District's recommendations.
Simpler Sentence: The Park District's recommendations are unclear.

AVOIDING CLUSTERS OF NOUNS

Clusters of nouns are groups of two or more nouns that together describe one thing. Noun clusters often crop up in planning documents. Sentences that have noun clusters can be difficult for readers to follow.

You can break up a noun cluster by using connecting words (such as "of," "in," or "for"), the possessive "'s," or verb forms of the nouns in the cluster. This usually results in a simpler (though sometimes longer) sentence.

Examples:

Noun Cluster Sentence: The city student population total is increasing faster than school district enrollment capacity.
Simpler Sentence: The number of students in the city is increasing faster than the school district's enrollment capacity.

In the above example, the first sentence has two clusters of nouns: "city student population total" and "school district enrollment capacity." The second sentence is slightly longer, but simplifies the message by using the connecting words "of" and "in" ("the number of students in the city") and the possessive "'s" ("the school district's enrollment capacity").

Here's another example:

Noun Cluster Sentence: This memo describes City use permit application review procedures.
Simpler Sentence: This memo describes the City's procedures for reviewing applications for use permits.

In the above example, the simpler sentence breaks up the noun cluster ("City use permit application review procedures") by using the possessive "'s" ("City's procedures"), the connecting word "for," and the verb form of one of the nouns ("review" becomes "reviewing").

EXERCISES

Reducing the Number of Ideas Per Sentence

Revise the following passages to reduce the number of ideas per sentence:

a. While water quality in San Francisco Bay has improved significantly since the 1960s, due largely to strict regulation of discharges from factories, sewage treatment plants, and automobiles, the Bay still contains unhealthy levels of many pollutants, and fish and wildlife habitats are being damaged.

b. The City Council adopted the ordinance in October, following which Planning Department staff identified a change that they believed to be necessary to one of the conditions, requiring the Council to review and adopt a revised ordinance in November.

c. The latest set of regional projections predict that, for the next 20 years, Stepford will continue to grow faster than the county as a whole, accounting for 60 percent of the county's growth between 2000 and 2020 (with 10,100 persons expected to be added to Stepford's population and only 17,100 to be added in the county as a whole). According to the projections, household sizes are expected to continue their downward trend, in Stepford and elsewhere in the county, but Stepford is seen as continuing to have a much larger typical household size than both the county and the region as a whole.

d. The development plan must be revised by the applicant to incorporate the tree protection measures established in the City's Tree Ordinance, and no exceptions to these measures will be allowed (i.e., no grading permit will be issued) unless justified to City satisfaction, based on a report by a qualified independent arborist retained by the City at applicant expense, that the trees are damaged and diseased.

Removing Extra Words

Reduce the number of words in the following sentences:

a. Because of the fact that the proposed project does not include an adequate number of parking spaces, it is probable that an excessive number of vehicles will seek parking within the public right-of-way.

b. The building moratorium will be in effect for a period of one year, during which time the City will conduct a study as to the effects of new development on traffic patterns as a means of identifying necessary road construction projects.

c. It is interesting to note that, in cases in which commercial facilities are located within one-half mile of residential uses, it can be anticipated that residents will in many instances choose to walk rather than drive to these facilities.

d. Citizens in many cases have questions in regard to whether there are cases in which use permits for second units can be approved by the Zoning Administrator, in lieu of the Planning Commission.

Avoiding Clusters of Nouns

Rewrite the following sentences to remove noun clusters:

a. At the next meeting, the City Council will review City road improvement fee collection procedures.

b. Park Department recreation programs are currently under review.

c. The Zoning Ordinance-required 20-foot front yard building setback applies to this property.

d. The City cannot make a general plan consistency finding unless the project meets the Park Ordinance trail/open space dedication requirements.

4

Writing Active Sentences

Consider this sentence: "It is the determination of City staff that there is a possibility of associated increases in traffic noise if this project is approved and constructed." It sounds bureaucratic and dull, doesn't it? It's also unclear. Who is going to approve the project? Who is going to construct it?

The sentence is "passive"; it uses the passive voice (in this case, the verb "is") and has several nouns that the writer could convert to verbs. Why are so many planning documents full of sentences like this? Perhaps we think that we cannot write about our subject in a lively way and still sound professional and objective. Sometimes, perhaps due to political pressure or just bureaucratic thinking, we deliberately avoid stating who is responsible for the actions we are writing about.

When you write in active sentences, your writing almost instantly becomes clearer, less bureaucratic, more specific, and more interesting. This is because active verbs are by nature livelier than passive ones. For example, you could rewrite the above sentence to read "City staff believes that traffic noise may increase if the County approves this project and the developer builds it as proposed." This sentence is shorter, livelier, and more specific about who is carrying out the action (in this case, a development approval and construction). Notice that the rewritten sentence clears up any confusion about who is approving the project (the County), and who will build it (the developer).

AVOIDING THE PASSIVE VOICE

Passive voice sentences usually have two basic features:

- a form of the verb "to be" (like "am," "is," "are," "was," "were," "be," or "been"), and

- a main verb usually ending in "en" or "ed."

Planning documents are usually full of sentences that needlessly use the passive voice. Here are some common examples.

The Ambiguous Sentence

By using the passive voice, the writer avoids identifying the subject of the sentence (that is, who or what is responsible for the action implied in the sentence). This use of the passive voice is the worst offender because the writing is not only dull, but often unclear.

Example:

Passive Sentence: A preliminary grading plan shall be submitted prior to project approval.
Active Sentence: The developer shall submit a grading plan prior to project approval.
or
The developer must submit a grading plan before the City approves the project.

Notice that the "passive voice" sentence does not specify who should submit the grading plan (or, for that matter, who will approve it). This type of ambiguity can cause problems when a reader–the planner in charge of the project, for example–tries to identify who is responsible for what. By writing the sentence in the active voice, you can make the sentence more specific by stating who (in this case, the developer) will carry out the action (in this case, submit a grading plan).

Some passive sentences do not tell us "who" because the "who" is not actually very important. Still, the writer is usually better off recasting the sentence to use the active voice.

Example:

Passive Sentence: The table is intended to identify maximum acceptable densities for different types of housing.
Active Sentence: The table lists maximum acceptable densities for different types of housing.

In this case, the passive sentence does not say who "intended" to identify the maximum acceptable densities, probably because it isn't necessary: It's the author who is doing the "intending." Notice that you can delete three extra words if you rewrite the sentence in an active voice, making "the table" the subject of the sentence.

The Lazy Sentence

Sometimes, a writer just gets lazy. Phrases that begin with the words "in" or "by" are often clues that the writer could easily turn the sentence around to read in the active voice.

Examples:

Passive Sentence: Existing contaminant levels at the project site are summarized in Table 5.
Active Sentence: Table 5 lists existing contaminant levels at the project site.

Passive Sentence: The location of the San Andreas Fault is illustrated by Figure 2.
Active Sentence: Figure 2 shows the location of the San Andreas Fault.

Possible Exceptions

Most of the time, it is preferable to write an "active voice" sentence that states who will do what when. In writing about planning matters, though, it sometimes isn't practical or appropriate to list every party that will be carrying out an action. The actors may be unknown, unimportant, obvious, or best left unidentified for political reasons. For example, if your main point is that a school/park site plan is forthcoming, you may not want to write that "the City, the School District, the Park District, and the current developer will work together to design a school/park site plan." The long list of parties carrying out the action may distract from the main point. It's also possible that you do not yet know who is going to design the site plan, or do not want to assign responsibility yet because the parties are still negotiating. In any of these cases, you may instead write that "a school/park site plan will be designed."

While the "active voice" is usually preferable, you need not force it into every sentence you write. You may want to use the "passive voice" at least sparingly to retain the continuity of a series of sentences. Here is an example:

The 30 proposed residential lots would range from five to 10 acres in size [active voice]. They would be clustered in groups of five to 10 lots [passive voice]. The lot clusters would be surrounded by undeveloped common areas [passive voice].

Rewriting the sentences to use only the active voice would produce a "choppier" description, like this:

The 30 proposed residential lots would range from five to 10 acres in size [active voice]. The applicant proposes to cluster them in groups of five to 10 lots [active voice]. Undeveloped common areas would surround the lot clusters [active voice].

This version uses only the active voice. It is also acceptable, but the ideas do not flow as smoothly here as they do in the first example.

TURNING NOUNS BACK INTO VERBS

Nouns created from verbs are common culprits in passive sentences. You can convert many of these nouns back into verbs to create shorter, clearer, and more active sentences.

Examples:

Passive Sentence: The requirement of the Zoning Ordinance is for a 25-foot-wide setback in the R-1 District.
Active Sentence: The Zoning Ordinance requires a 25-foot-wide setback in the R-1 District.

Passive Sentence: The objective of the committee is the establishment of citywide planning goals.
Active Sentence: The committee will establish citywide planning goals.

Passive Sentence: It is the determination of City staff that the project is inconsistent with the General Plan.
Active Sentence: City staff has determined that the project is inconsistent with the General Plan.

Passive Sentence: There is a possibility of City Council denial of this application.
Active Sentence: The City Council may deny this application.

In these examples, you can write more active sentences by converting the nouns "requirement," "establishment," "determination," and "denial" into the verbs "require," "establish," "determine," and "deny."

Table 2 lists some of the noun-based sentence constructions that planners commonly use, and the verbs you may try using instead.

Table 2
✶ TURNING NOUNS BACK INTO VERBS

Instead of:	*Try:*
establish a requirement	require
give consideration to	consider
give recognition to	recognize
issue an approval	approve
issue a denial	deny
make a determination	determine
make a distribution	distribute
make a payment	pay
make a recommendation	recommend
provide information	inform
submit an application	apply
take an action	act

EXERCISES

Avoiding the Passive Voice

Convert the following sentences from the passive voice to the active voice:

a. This report is intended to inform readers as to the general plan preparation process.

b. Existing land uses in the area are illustrated by Map 1.

c. A habitat management plan shall be prepared and submitted to the City by the applicant for review and approval by the City prior to issuance of a grading permit for a project.

d. The federal and state standards are shown in Table 10 for key pollutants.

e. City Council approval of this project could most likely be expected to encourage similar rezoning requests in the future.

f. The citizens advisory committee's recommendations are described in this report.

g. Our grant application was not approved by the foundation board of directors.

Turning Nouns Back Into Verbs

Make the following sentences more active by converting key nouns to verbs:

a. Distribution of the public notice by the County included interested citizens.

b. In deciding whether to issue an approval for the project, the Planning Commission gave consideration to the project's consistency with the City's general plan policies on affordable housing.

c. The recommendation of design guidelines is the committee's top priority.

d. The property owner is proposing a lot line adjustment that would result in reconfiguration and consolidation of the ten existing lots into two new lots.

e. State law has established a requirement that developers make "impact fee" payments to affected school districts.

f. The Zoning Administrator has issued a determination that this project does not meet the criteria for approval of a variance.

CHAPTER 5

Using Simple Words
and Avoiding Jargon

Y ou have probably seen something like this in movies:
A doctor is explaining a medical situation to his pa-
tient's distraught family. The doctor is using lots of
complicated words, and the family is getting more and
more upset, until finally a family friend jumps in: "She has
a bad case of the flu." Everyone understands this explanation; it's direct and to-the-point. And predictably the doctor–the highly trained expert, the person who actually
knows the most–ends up looking ineffective and a little
silly.

Planners' jargon doesn't usually make people so upset,
probably because our work doesn't affect them in quite
such a personal way. But planning does involve their property, their communities, the views out their windows–emo-
tional issues for most people. Planners are often called
upon to explain to property owners why the horse stable in
their backyard needs a use permit, or why the 10 disman-

tled autos in their front yard are a blight and a hazard, or why the housing development proposed next door is consistent with city plans. Like doctors, we would probably make a better impression if we communicated without jargon.

RECOGNIZING JARGON

The best way to recognize jargon in your writing is to imagine that you are speaking directly to one of your readers, or better yet to a friend–someone who is reasonably intelligent but who may not know a lot about your subject. How would you convey your ideas if this person were sitting across a table from you? Would you use the same words? The words that seem too complicated, pompous, or formal for that situation are probably the jargon words.

Examples:

Jargon Sentence: Grading activity required by new development would have associated short-term erosion impacts.
Plain English Sentence: Grading would cause soil to erode.

Jargon Sentence: Project traffic activity would impact regional air quality.
Plain English Sentence: Project traffic would emit carbon monoxide, worsening air pollution in the region.

The jargon sentences above include the words "activity" and "impact"–two jargon words that usually appear too often in planning documents. The second jargon sentence uses the word "impact" as a verb; in addition to being jargon-y, this is grammatically incorrect, since the word "impact" is a noun, not a verb.

Jargon Sentence: Public infrastructure can be growth-inducing from a local and regional perspective.
Plain English Sentences: Construction of streets, sidewalks, and water and sewer pipes would allow development plans for the area to move ahead. Development in this area could bring changes throughout the region.

Just a few jargon words can cloud the meaning of an entire sentence. In the above example, notice how removing the terms "infrastructure," "growth-inducing," and "perspective" forces the writer to convey the idea more clearly. (Of course, that can mean using more words, as the example shows.)

Table 3 lists only some of the most common planning jargon. Substituting the simpler words can make your writing clearer and more specific.

Table 3
AVOIDING JARGON

Instead of:	*Try:*
activity	(be more specific, or remove)
agendize	put on the agenda
buffer	area, strip, separation
commercial land use	store, shop, business
conceptualize	draft, design, suggest, write
corridor (as in "view corridor," "road corridor," "riparian corridor")	area, view, road, creek
dwelling unit	house, apartment
effect (as in "noise effect," "odor effect," "traffic effect")	noise, odor, traffic
empirical	first-hand (or remove)
impact (noun) (as in "noise impact," "odor impact," "traffic impact")	noise, odor, traffic
impact (when used incorrectly as a verb)	damage, destroy, set back, change
implement (verb)	build, enforce, apply, carry out, start
improvement (as in "road improvement")	road, road construction, road widening

incremental	gradual, step-by-step
infrastructure	water, sewer, storm drainage, roads, etc. (specify)
mitigate	reduce, avoid, prevent
negative traffic impacts	traffic congestion, traffic jam
neighborhood commercial establishment	store, shop, business
paradigm	model, rule, idea (or remove)
parameter	limit, boundary, rule, guideline
pedestrian furniture	benches
plant material	plants
prioritize	rank, set priorities
prototypical	model, sample, example, original
residence	house, apartment
residential land uses	houses, apartments, housing
roadway	road
transportation facilities	roads, buses
urban fabric	character, appearance

Possible Exceptions

Note that jargon can be useful as shorthand, as long as all of your readers will understand it. If you are writing a memo to a colleague, for example, using jargon might be acceptable. Most of the time, though, our readers include people who are not planners, so our writing should be understandable to them.

When you are writing for a general audience, you may sometimes need to use a technical term to convey an idea accurately and precisely. Consider carefully, though, whether you could use a more common word instead; many planning ideas translate into simple language. If you do choose the technical term, explain what it means when you first use it.

Many planning documents, including general plans, zoning ordinances, and environmental impact reports, routinely use jargon words like those listed in Table 3, sometimes because the terms come from an applicable law. (The words "impact," "effect," and "mitigation," for example, are a staple of many environmental documents because the National Environmental Policy Act, the California Environmental Quality Act, and other laws use these terms.) If you are working with these documents, you might not be able to avoid using their jargon. Perhaps you can use the words sparingly, or quote the jargon-riddled passages as they appear in the document. You can then explain what they mean, or provide a glossary that defines the more difficult terms. The idea is to avoid using jargon when you don't have to.

Strange as it may seem, there are times when writing jargon-free text may stir up trouble. When you use plain language, people might become angry, upset, or offended simply because they understand what you are actually trying to say, or because you are saying it differently from how others have. While this happens more often than you might imagine, it doesn't necessarily mean that you should avoid writing clearly. In fact, the trouble you've stirred may ultimately be worthwhile. A true story illustrates this point.

When Plain Language Makes People Mad: A True Story

A private school was seeking to build a new campus in a well-to-do community. The site that the school chose had a pond that was home to an endangered species of frog. In an early draft of the environmental impact report (EIR) on the school, the EIR biologist identified the following as a possible "project impact":

Interactions between student and frog, ranging from placing frogs in teachers' desk drawers to harassing frogs via stone throwing, are a long-standing phenomenon and may occur at the project site once the new school is in operation.

This seems like a reasonable, and even slightly whimsical, statement of the problem, doesn't it? Nonetheless, upon reading this sentence in the first draft of the EIR, school representatives were quite upset at the suggestion that their students would misbehave in this way. After some debate with the school people and with the city's Planning Department staff (who were the EIR client), the EIR consultants rewrote the offending sentence as follows:

The project would bring human occupants (students, faculty, and visitors) to the site, increasing the possibility of interactions with and harassment of the frog.

The rewritten sentence may be more objective and less inflammatory, but it certainly lacks the specificity and punch of the early statement. If the biologist had written the sentence this way in the first place, it probably would have gone unnoticed. It's also possible, though, that no one would have thought about the point that the biologist was trying to make. As it turned out, the process of revising that one sentence illuminated a variety of possible solutions to the frog harassment problem, such as requiring the school not only to install a fence around the pond, but also to provide nature education for the students.

What are the lessons? "Know your readers" (see Part I of this book) might be one. (It's possible that public school and local government representatives in a less affluent community would not be quite so sensitive to allegations of misbehavior by students.) Let's assume that "write in jargon so that people won't understand what you're talking about" isn't another. In fact, by writing the sentence first in plain language, the biologist made sure that the problem was out on the table for discussion, even though some people may have been offended. And sometimes sticking with the clear, jargon-free statement may be the best (and possibly even the ethical) thing to do, regardless of whether someone may be offended.

AVOIDING ACRONYMS

Acronyms are a special and increasingly common type of jargon. An acronym consists of the first letters of the words it represents. Common examples in planning documents include the names of agencies (like "GUSD" for "Gotham Unified School District"), laws (like "NEPA" for "National Environmental Policy Act"), programs (like "NPDES" for "National Pollution Discharge Elimination System"), and technical terms (like "sf" for "square feet"). Acronyms can be difficult for readers to understand and remember.

Consider whether you really need to use an acronym, or whether you can use the complete term ("Gotham Unified School District") or a shortened version of it ("the District") instead. If you will be using the term only a few times, write it out each time instead of using an acronym. If you do use an acronym, write out the term in full with the acronym in parentheses the first time you use it—"Gotham Unified School District (GUSD)"—then use the acronym ("GUSD") consistently throughout the rest of the text.

If you must use acronyms and other technical terms, consider including a glossary in your document. Take care, though, not to think of the glossary as an excuse for using more technical terms than necessary. For example, in describing the results of a noise study, you may not be able to avoid using the term "CNEL"; in that case, define "Community Noise Equivalent Level" in the glossary. Before you add the term "du" to the glossary, though, consider whether you could just say "dwelling unit"–or better yet, "house"–instead.

What if you run across an undefined acronym and you don't know the complete name or term? The glossary at the end of this book lists acronyms commonly used in the planning field. Consult this list, or glossaries in other reference sources, for translations. If you still come up short, ask the authors of the document you are reviewing, or other colleagues. (Don't be embarrassed–they might appreciate learning that not everyone is familiar with a term they thought was common.)

FINDING THE SIMPLER WORD

Some words that clutter planning documents do not qualify as planning jargon. These words are not specific to our profession, but they are still unnecessarily complicated. It's generally best to replace these words with shorter, more common ones.

Examples:

Complicated Words: The property is located contiguous to the airport and comprises 30 acres.

Simpler Words: The 30-acre property is located next to the airport.

Complicated Words: The Planning Department utilized newspaper ads to disseminate further information concerning the General Plan update.
Simpler Words: The Planning Department used newspaper ads to issue more information about the General Plan update.

Complicated Words: The developer's acreage calculations frequently contain a substantial number of errors.
Simpler Words: The developer's acreage calculations often have many errors.

Table 4 lists simpler words that might replace the all-too-common complicated ones.

Possible Exceptions

More complicated words are sometimes preferable to simpler ones because they set a more formal and less inflammatory tone. For example, if you are writing a letter to tell someone that they are violating a zoning ordinance regulation, you may want to tell them that they "must cease hog-raising operations within 30 days," rather than that they "must stop raising hogs in the backyard within 30 days." A slightly more formal tone may also be desirable as a way of conveying the importance of a document like a general plan. Do try, though, to strike a balance between setting the right tone and making your writing less bureaucratic and easier to understand. Most of the complicated words in Table 4 are very much overused. The simpler ones are usually better.

Table 4
FINDING THE SIMPLER WORD

Instead of:	*Try:*
accomplish	carry out, do
accordingly	so
accrue	add, gain
accurate	correct, exact, right
additional	added, more, other
address (verb)	discuss
adjacent to	next to
afford	allow, let
allocate	divide, give
anticipate	expect
a number of	some, many (or specify number)
apparent	clear, plain
appropriate	(omit), proper, right
approximately	about

ascertain	find out, learn
assist, assistance	aid, help
attain	meet
attempt (verb)	try
benefit	help
capability	ability, can
cease	stop
close proximity	near
commence	begin, start
complete (verb)	finish
comply with	follow, meet
component	part
comprise	form, include, make up
concept	idea
concerning	about, on
consequence	result
consequently	so
consolidate	combine, join, merge
constitutes	is, forms, makes up
contain	have
contiguous to	next to
currently	(omit), now

demonstrate	prove, show
determine	decide, figure, find
disseminate	give, issue, pass, send, provide
eliminate	cut, drop, end, prevent, remove
employ	use
equitable	fair
equivalent	equal
evidenced	showed, shown
evident	clear
exhibit	show
expedite	hasten, speed up
expertise	ability, skill
expiration	end
facilitate	aid, ease, help
failed to	did not
feasible	can be done, workable, possible
finalize	complete, finish
following	after
formulate	write, draft
forthwith	immediately

forward	send
frequently	often
function	act, role, work
furnish	give, send
further (adjective)	more
herein	here
heretofore	until now
herewith	below, here
however	but, though
identical	same
initiate, commence	start, begin
indicate	show
inform	tell
institute	begin, start
interface with	meet, work with
manner	way
maximum	most, largest, greatest
minimum	least, smallest
modify	change
necessitate	require
portion	part
possess	have

principal	main, key, important
prior	earlier
prior to	before
proceed	go, go ahead, start, begin
pursuant to	under
regarding	about
remainder	rest
render ("cause to be")	make
render ("give")	give
require ("need")	need
retain	keep
revision/revise	change
specified	named
subsequent to	after
substantial	large
sufficient	enough
terminate	end
upon	on
utilize	use

Source: Plain Language Action Network; National Archives and Records Administration, Office of the Federal Register.

EXERCISES

Remove the jargon and other complicated words and terms from the following sentences:

a. As demonstrated in the illustration, the proposed new building would significantly impact the Broadway view corridor.

b. The roadway widening improvement project needs to be completed prior to commencement of building construction.

c. Small-scale ground floor commercial uses such as groceries, restaurants, and other businesses with upper floor residential uses characterize the neighborhood's dense urban fabric.

d. The building rehabilitation program will facilitate implementation of general plan policies concerning historic preservation in this portion of the downtown area.

e. A 50-foot-wide buffer comprised of native trees and plant materials will be utilized to separate the dwelling units contiguous to the roadway from the roadway.

f. The information concerning the project disseminated by the developer prior to the public hearing failed to eliminate citizen opposition.

g. The proposed public open space plaza area would include lawn and table facilities for passive recreational activities such as picnicking and sunbathing.

h. Recognizing that we have special expertise in park planning, the client has consequently requested that we formulate park design concept guidelines to mitigate safety impacts.

i. The Public Works Department staff will interface with Planning Department staff to render a decision in regards to which front yard setback requirement applies in this case prior to building permit issuance.

6

Explaining Technical Information

One of our more difficult writing tasks as planners is to explain scientific or other technical information to a general audience. Often, this involves translating the jargon of many other fields (including law, architecture, traffic engineering, geology, biology, hydrology, and acoustics) into plain language. To do this well, we need to think even more carefully about our readers: How much do they need to know about the subject? What is the best way to explain it? What is the main message?

To anticipate our readers' needs in this way, we must understand the subject well enough to write about it clearly. Unfortunately, this sometimes means asking what seem like dumb questions of the specialists we are working with. It's always worth remembering that if we don't understand it, chances are our readers won't either.

EXPLAINING PROCESSES FROM THE BEGINNING

Planners often find themselves writing about a process, whether it is an environmental process or a governmental one. When explaining a process, it's usually best to start at the beginning, so that someone who is unfamiliar with the process can follow the train of thought.

Example:

Hard-to-Follow Sentence: During the project construction phase when trenches are excavated, trench wall instability may exist.

A reader unfamiliar with the land development process might not know what these trenches are, or what "trench wall instability" means.

Clearer Sentences: During project construction, utility companies would excavate trenches for water and sewer pipes. In areas with weaker soils, the walls of these trenches may be unstable.

This explanation uses more words, but is easier for most readers to understand.

HIGHLIGHTING THE MAIN POINT

As planners, we often serve as intermediaries between technical specialists and the public. In this role, one of our most important tasks is to wade through technical information and find the main point.

Example:

Unclear Point: The sampling of reservoir water, completed under high suspended sediment conditions, shows detectable amounts of mercury (1.05 to 1.74 ppm).

While a hydrologist has supplied what may be very valuable information, most readers will probably not understand the significance of this statement. The sentence also probably does not convey the main point for planning purposes.

Clearer Point: People who use the reservoir for swimming or other recreation may be exposed to mercury in reservoir water and sediment. A sampling of reservoir water found that mercury levels exceeded accepted standards.

In this explanation, the writer has used the scientific data to explain the planning concern: Mercury in the reservoir may be a hazard to human health. Readers may not need to know exactly how high the mercury levels were. The writer could go on to explain the data, if necessary.

USING SPECIFIC EXAMPLES

One of the best ways to liven up complicated or dry information is to provide a specific example. This can require a bit more work on your part, but is often well worth the effort.

Example:

General Sentence: This intersection operates at Level of Service F during the PM peak hour.

Specific Sentences: Between 5:00 and 6:00 PM, there are long lines of cars waiting to cross this intersection. Drivers typically wait through more than one green light before entering the intersection. Traffic engineers define these conditions as "Level of Service F." Like a school report card, the Level of Service measurement ranks intersection operations on a scale ranging from "A" (best possible performance) to "F" (worst possible performance, or "flunking").

EXERCISES

Explaining Processes from the Beginning

Rewrite the following sentences so that they explain the process from the beginning:

a. The City Council must take an action on the development application by this October 1 in order to meet the one-year requirements of state law, since the application was submitted on October 1 of last year.

b. If traffic levels at the intersection justify installation of a traffic signal, a signal will be installed after traffic monitoring conducted by the City after the housing units are constructed and occupied demonstrates the need for the signal.

c. The creek currently contains little plant or animal life because water quality in the creek becomes degraded when pollutants such as oil and grease carried by storm water enter the creek from automobiles and other vehicles that park on paved surfaces such as roads and parking lots.

d. The Acme Product Foundation's revised applications for general plan amendment and rezoning were filed in late 1999, and were preceded by the original general plan amendment application in late 1990, which was followed by the original rezoning application in early 1991–applications that the City denied in the spring of 1991.

Highlighting the Main Point

(Note: The "main point" will very much depend on the circumstances, of course, and on the concerns of your readers. Use these exercises merely to think about how to summarize and extract a main point out of large amounts of information.)

a. Based on the current Police Department standard of one officer per 1,000 residents, the proposed housing development would generate a need for five sworn personnel. The project would also create a need for support staff. Based on the General Plan police facility standard of 150 square feet of station area per 1,000 residents, the project would create a need for approximately 2,000 square feet of station area, requiring construction of a new substation. A new beat staffed by additional personnel would be created by the Police Department to meet the five-minute response time for suburban areas called for by General Plan policy 5-10. The project would also create a need for one vehicle for every two sworn staff, and additional equipment.

b. One factor that the City Council should consider in deciding whether to extend the urban limit line is that lands in this area are rated Class I and Class II by the U.S. Department of Agriculture, indicating that they have the fewest limitations for agricultural use. Class I and Class II soils are defined as "prime soils" that could support a range of different crop types, including apples, walnuts, corn, tomatoes, and others, assuming that the lands are irrigated. The lands in the area in question are irrigated, and in 1989 300 acres were planted with an apple orchard that has been productive since that year and is still in operation.

c. Surf City currently contains approximately 6,000 employed residents. The number of employed residents is projected to increase to 15,000 in 10 years, and 19,000 in 20 years. Meanwhile, the number of jobs in the city, currently set at 4,000, is expected to increase to 11,000 in 10 years and 15,000 in 20 years. The ratio of employed residents to jobs is currently 1.50 (i.e., one job for every 1.5 residents), and will be 1.36 in 10 years and 1.27 in 20 years, suggesting that, while proportionately more residents may be able to work in Surf City in the future, there will continue to be more residents than jobs in the city, and some people will have to commute elsewhere for jobs.

d. Under the current General Plan policy (Policy 7.7), approval of the density bonus aspect of the project must be contingent on a park dedication that the City Council determines is sufficient to override the approximately 100-acre loss of open space. The 100-acre open space area currently contains oak woodland habitat. Such an action would be expected to result in similar requests for density bonuses in exchange for park dedications on other surrounding rural residential lands, which are currently developed at a density of approximately one housing unit per 20 acres. If the density bonus is approved by the Council without requiring the park dedication, then the Council may be compelled to make similar density bonus concessions to other property owners.

Using Lists

Planning documents use lists in many ways. Examples include:

- objectives, goals, and policies in a plan,
- conditions of approval for a development project,
- requirements for an application submittal, and
- recommendations for a planning commission action.

As the above paragraph shows, a list can be a good way to present a lengthy series of related ideas. Without the bullets, the paragraph might read like this:

Planning documents use lists in many ways. Objectives, goals, and policies in a plan are one example. Conditions of approval for a development project are another. So are requirements for an application submittal, and recommendations for a planning commission action.

The paragraph isn't unreadable, but the bulleted version is clearer, isn't it?

USING BULLETS

When a sentence or paragraph includes a list of related items, using bullets can set off the information more clearly in the text. Here are some guidelines for using bullets:[1]

- Make sure that the items on the list are related,
- Check that the items are in "parallel construction" (i.e., grammatical structure and verb tense are consistent from bullet to bullet),
- Make sure that each item would form a complete sentence with the "lead-in,"
- Make sure that the lead-in contains all ideas common to all items,
- Use numbers instead of bullets when describing a step-by-step procedure,
- Use consistent punctuation,
- If the list consists of alternatives, put "or" after the second-to-last item, and
- If the list is inclusive, put "and" after the second-to-last item.

Examples:

Incorrect Use of Bullets:
When you submit your use permit application:
- Provide 10 copies of the completed application.
- Include 10 copies of your written project description, and
- 10 copies of your project plans should be included.

In the above example, the bulleted items are not in "parallel construction"; the first two bullets are commands, while the third bullet uses the "should be" construction. The punctuation is not consistent; the first bullet ends with a period, while the second bullet uses a comma. The requirement for 10 copies can be moved to the lead-in, since it is common to all three items.

Better Use of Bullets:
Your use permit application should include 10 copies each of:
- the completed application,
- your written project description, and
- your project plans.

Possible Exceptions

It is possible to overuse bullets. Make sure that you want to call attention to the items in your list before you present them in bullet form. If it does not seem especially useful to list the items separately, discuss them in paragraph form instead.

---

1. Plain Language Action Network, "Plain Train–Plain Language Online Training Program" (available at www.plainlanguage.gov).

WRITING POLICIES AND CONDITIONS

The guidelines for bulleted items also apply to goals, objectives, policies, programs, and conditions. Non-parallel construction is a common problem with these types of lists.

Examples:

Non-Parallel Construction:
Goal 1. Protect wetlands from urban development.
Goal 2. Prime agricultural lands shall be preserved.

Parallel Construction:
Goal 1. Protect wetlands from urban development.
Goal 2. Preserve prime agricultural lands.

Non-parallel construction can create confusion, for example between what is a policy (and therefore advisory) and what is a program (requiring an action). Here is an example:

Non-Parallel Construction:
Policy 1. Use Planned Development (PD) zoning to encourage more varied housing developments.
Program 1.1. The Town of Bedrock will rezone the Northern Quarry area from R-1 (Single-Family Residential) to PD.
Policy 2. The Town of Bedrock shall consider allowing density bonuses for housing projects that reserve units for low-income households.

Program 2.1. The Town will encourage development of an affordable housing program.

In the above example, the non-parallel construction between Policy 1 and Policy 2 is a clue that the writer has gotten the policies and programs mixed up. A rewrite using parallel construction solves the problem.

Parallel Construction:
Policy 1. Use Planned Development (PD) zoning to encourage more varied housing developments.
Program 1.1. The Town of Bedrock will rezone the Northern Quarry area from R-1 (Single-Family Residential) to PD.
Policy 2. Encourage development of affordable housing.
Program 2.1. The Town will adopt an affordable housing program that allows density bonuses for housing projects that reserve units for low-income households.

You should also choose your verbs carefully when writing these types of requirements. Table 5 lists "auxiliary" verbs that planners commonly use in conditions and policy statements. In particular, you might consider avoiding "shall," a dull, legal-style word that is not often used in everyday speech. "Shall" can also be ambiguous; it can convey either an obligation ("you shall do this") or an intent or prediction ("I shall do this"). Try using "must" instead. (Be aware, though, that to some people in the planning field, and to virtually all lawyers and judges, the idea of abandoning the word "shall" will seem revolutionary.)

Table 5
USING THE RIGHT VERB IN CONDITIONS AND POLICIES

Use:	*If You Want to:*
must	require something
may	allow something
should	indicate preference for something (but not require it absolutely)
will	predict something
shall	(consider avoiding, since meaning can be confused with "must" and "will")

EXERCISES

Using Bullets

Convert the following paragraphs to bulleted lists:

a. City staff recommends that the Planning Commission certify the environmental document as adequate and complete. The Commission should also recommend approval of the proposed general plan amendment and rezoning by the City Council.

b. The developer should hire a qualified geologist to prepare a detailed map of landslides on the site. The geologist should complete a detailed analysis of the unstable areas on the sites of the proposed buildings. The analysis should identify areas that would be inappropriate for mass grading, and measures to reduce hazards in areas where grading would be appropriate.

c. The Zoning Ordinance requires a 20-foot front yard setback. It requires a 20-foot rear yard setback and a 5-foot side yard setback.

d. Areas of the site, including the graded hillside, the proposed classroom buildings, the proposed library building, the proposed soccer field, the proposed tennis courts, and the main entry road and emergency access road, would be visible from the freeway.

Improve the format of the following bulleted lists, using the guidelines suggested in this chapter:

e. After you submit your application, County staff will:
   • Review it to make sure it is complete,
   • Schedule the application for a Planning Commission hearing;
   • Staff will send you a letter notifying you of the hearing date.

f. The R-1 zoning requires that:
   • A maximum building height of 30 feet;
   • A minimum front yard setback of 20 feet,
   • Minimum side yard setbacks are five feet.

Writing Policies and Conditions

Correct the format problems in the following examples:

a. **Policy 1:** Encourage mixed use development.
   Program 1.1: The City will revise the Zoning Ordinance to allow residential uses in the Neighborhood Commercial zone.

   Policy 2: The City shall encourage development of housing in the downtown.
   Program 2.1: Rezone Hampshire Street between Fifth and Tenth Streets to allow mixed use (residential/commercial) development.

b. **Condition 1:** The applicant shall pay all applicable school impact fees before applying for a grading permit.
   Condition 2: The applicant should install all required landscaping before applying for a certificate of occupancy.

c. **Policy 1:** Protect scenic views to the extent possible.
   Program 1.1: Develop and enforce guidelines for development along scenic routes.

   Policy 2: Prominent hillsides and other important natural features shall be preserved.
   Program 2.1: The City shall adopt guidelines for hillside grading.

Exercise Key

Please note: *The "answers" provided here are not necessarily the only acceptable ones. You may find other solutions that are as good as–or better than–these suggestions. In writing, as in planning, there is often more than one reasonable way to solve a problem.*

WRITING SIMPLE SENTENCES

Reducing the Number of Ideas Per Sentence

a. Water quality in San Francisco Bay has improved significantly since the 1960s. This has largely been due to strict regulation of discharges from factories, sewage treatment plants, and automobiles. Nonetheless, the Bay still has unhealthy levels of many pollutants. These high pollutant levels are damaging fish and wildlife habitats.

b. The City Council adopted the ordinance in October. Planning Department staff later identified a necessary change to one of the conditions. This required the Council to review and adopt a revised ordinance in November.

c. The latest regional projections predict that, for the next 20 years, Stepford will continue to grow faster than the county as a whole. Between 2000 and 2020, Stepford's population increase (10,100 people) will represent 60 percent of the county's growth (17,100 people). The projections show that household sizes will continue to decrease, in Stepford and elsewhere in the county. The typical household in Stepford will continue to be much larger than households in both the county and the region as a whole, however.

d. The applicant must revise the development plan to incorporate the tree protection measures established in the City's Tree Ordinance. The City will not issue a grading permit until the applicant submits a development plan that complies with these measures. The City will not allow exceptions to these measures unless an arborist report shows that the trees are damaged or diseased. The City will retain a qualified arborist, at applicant expense, to prepare the arborist report.

Removing Extra Words

a. Because the proposed project does not provide enough parking spaces, the demand for on-street parking will probably exceed supply.

or

Because the proposed project does not provide enough parking spaces, drivers will probably compete for limited on-street parking.

b. The building moratorium will be in effect for one year, while the City studies projected traffic from future development to identify necessary road construction projects.

or

The building moratorium will be in effect for one year, while the City identifies road construction projects necessary to accommodate traffic from future development.

c. Residents will often walk, rather than drive, to shops located within one-half mile of home.

d. Citizens often have questions about when the Zoning Administrator, rather than the Planning Commission, can approve use permits for second units.

Avoiding Clusters of Nouns

a. At the next meeting, the City Council will review the City's procedures for collecting fees for road improvements.

or

At the next meeting, the City Council will review the City's procedures for collecting road improvement fees.

b. The Park Department's recreation programs are currently under review.

or

The Park Department is reviewing its recreation programs.

c. The Zoning Ordinance requires a front yard building set-back of 20 feet on this property.

or

The Zoning Ordinance requires that buildings on this property be set back 20 feet from the street.

or

The Zoning Ordinance requires that buildings on this property be set back 20 feet from the front property line.

d. The City cannot find the project consistent with the general plan unless the project meets the Park Ordinance's requirements for dedication of trails and open space.

WRITING ACTIVE SENTENCES

Avoiding the Passive Voice

a. This report informs readers about the general plan preparation process.

or

This report describes the general plan preparation process.

or

This report describes the process for preparing the general plan.

b. Map 1 illustrates existing land uses in the area.

c. The applicant shall prepare and submit a habitat management plan for City approval. The City shall review and approve the plan before issuing a grading permit for the project.

d. Table 10 shows federal and state standards for key pollutants.

e. City Council approval will most likely encourage similar rezoning requests in the future.

f. This report describes the citizens advisory committee's recommendations.

g. The foundation board of directors denied our grant application.

Turning Nouns Back into Verbs

a. The County distributed the public notice to interested citizens.

b. In deciding whether to approve the project, the Planning Commission considered whether the project is consistent with the City's general plan policies on affordable housing.

c. The committee's top priority is to recommend design guidelines.

d. The property owner is proposing a lot line adjustment to reconfigure and consolidate the 10 existing lots into two new lots.

or

The property owner is proposing to adjust the lot lines to reconfigure and consolidate the 10 existing lots into two new lots.

e. State law requires that developers pay "impact fees" to affected school districts.

f. The Zoning Administrator has determined that this project does not meet the criteria for approving a variance.

USING SIMPLE WORDS AND AVOIDING JARGON

a. As the illustration shows, the proposed new building would significantly change views down Broadway.

b. The road widening must be finished before building construction begins.

c. Small groceries, restaurants, and other businesses on the ground floor, with apartments above, give the neighborhood a dense, urban character.

d. The building rehabilitation program will help carry out general plan policies for historic preservation in this part of downtown.

e. A 50-foot-wide strip landscaped with native trees and plants will separate the houses from the adjoining road.

f. The information about the project that the developer sent out before the public hearing did not prevent citizen opposition.

g. The proposed public plaza would have picnic tables and lawns for sunbathing.

h. Because we have special skills in park planning, the client has requested that we draft guidelines for safe park design.

i. Before issuing a building permit, the Public Works Department staff will meet with Planning Department staff to decide which front yard setback requirement applies.

EXPLAINING TECHNICAL INFORMATION

Explaining Processes from the Beginning

a. State law requires that the City act on a development application within one year of receiving it. The City received this application on October 1 of last year. The City Council therefore must act on the application by this October 1.

b. After the housing is built and occupied, the City will monitor traffic at the intersection and will install a traffic signal if traffic is heavy enough to warrant it.

c. Automobiles and other vehicles leak oil and grease onto paved surfaces such as roads and parking lots. When it rains, the storm water washes these pollutants into the creek. The pollutants degrade water quality and make it difficult for plants and wildlife to survive in the creek. For this reason, the creek currently has little plant or animal life.

d. The Acme Product Foundation filed its original general plan amendment application in late 1990 and its original rezoning application in early 1991. The City denied these applications in the spring of 1991. The foundation filed revised applications for general plan amendment and rezoning in late 1999.

Highlighting the Main Point

a. The proposed housing development would create a need for five new police officers (plus support staff, vehicles, and equipment) and a new police substation. The Police Department would create a new beat staffed by the new officers to ensure that the Department could respond to service calls from the development within five minutes.

b. In deciding whether to extend the urban limit line, the City Council should consider the suitability and productivity of agricultural lands in this area. The U.S.

Department of Agriculture classifies these lands as prime agricultural soils. The lands are irrigated, and 300 acres have been producing apples since 1989.

c. Today, Surf City has more employed residents than jobs. Although job growth will start to catch up with the growth in employed residents over the next 10 to 20 years, Surf City will continue to have more employed residents than jobs. This means that some residents will have to commute to jobs outside the city.

d. Under the current General Plan policy, the City Council may only approve the density bonus for the project by finding that the project would provide a park that compensates for the loss of open space. If the Council approves the density bonus without requiring dedication of a park, then the Council may have to make similar concessions to other property owners in the future.

USING LISTS

Using Bullets

a. City staff recommends that the Planning Commission:
   • Certify the environmental document as adequate and complete, and
   • Recommend that the City Council approve the proposed general plan amendment and rezoning.

b. The developer should hire a qualified geologist to:
- prepare a detailed map of landslides on the site,
- analyze in detail the unstable areas where buildings are proposed,
- identify areas that would be inappropriate for mass grading, and
- recommend measures to reduce hazards in areas where grading would be appropriate.

c. The Zoning Ordinance requires the following setbacks:
- 20 feet in front yards and rear yards, and
- 5 feet in side yards.

or

The Zoning Ordinance requires the following setbacks:
- 20 feet in front yards,
- 20 feet in rear yards, and
- 5 feet in side yards.

d. Areas of the site that would be visible from the freeway include:
- the graded hillside,
- the proposed classroom buildings,
- the proposed library building,
- the proposed soccer field,
- the proposed tennis courts, and
- the main entry road and emergency access road.

e. After you submit your application, County staff will:
1. Review it to make sure it is complete,
2. Schedule the application for a Planning Commission hearing, and
3. Send you a letter notifying you of the hearing date.

f. The R-1 zoning requires:
  • A maximum building height of 30 feet,
  • A minimum front yard setback of 20 feet, and
  • Minimum side yard setbacks of five feet.
or
  The R-1 zoning specifies that buildings must be:
  • No higher than 30 feet,
  • Set back at least 20 feet from the front property line, and
  • Set back at least five feet from the side property lines.

Writing Policies and Conditions

a. **Policy 1:** Encourage mixed use development.
  Program 1.1: The City will revise the Zoning Ordinance to allow residential uses in the Neighborhood Commercial zone.
  Policy 2: Encourage development of housing in the downtown area.
  Program 2.1: The City will rezone Hampshire Street between Fifth and Tenth Streets to allow mixed use (residential/commercial) development.

b. **Condition 1:** The applicant must pay all applicable school impact fees before applying for a grading permit.
  Condition 2: The applicant must install all required landscaping before applying for a certificate of occupancy.

c. **Policy 1:** Protect scenic views to the extent possible.
Program 1.1: The City will develop and enforce guidelines for development along scenic routes.

Policy 2: Preserve prominent hillsides and other important natural features.
Program 2.1: The City will adopt guidelines for hillside grading.

References and Bibliography

BOOKS AND ARTICLES

Chan, Janis Fisher, and Diane Lutovich, *Professional Writing Skills: A Self-Paced Training Program*, Advanced Communication Designs, Inc., San Anselmo, Calif., second edition, 1997. A guide to business writing. Includes exercises.

Dandekar, Hemelata C. (editor), *The Planner's Use of Information*, Planners Press, American Planning Association, 1988. Contains a chapter on "Written Communications" that covers memos, letters, proposals, and reports. Includes exercises.

Leach, John, "Seven Steps to Better Writing," *Planning* magazine, June 1993. A concise review of planners' writing quirks.

Strunk, William Jr., and E.B. White, *The Elements of Style*, MacMillan Publishing Co., Inc., New York, third edition, 1979. The classic guide to clear writing.

Wydick, Richard C., *Plain English for Lawyers*, Carolina Academic Press, Durham, North Carolina, 1979. Suggests remedies for long, passive-voice sentences, complicated words, and other questionable writing habits that planners and lawyers share. Includes exercises.

INTERNET RESOURCES

The following documents are available at the web site address www.plainlanguage.gov, sponsored by the Plain Language Action

Network, a group that is working to improve federal government communications. Some of these documents provided background material for this book.

National Archives and Records Administration, Office of the Federal Register, "Drafting Legal Documents."

Office of Investor Education and Assistance, U.S. Securities and Exchange Commission, "A Plain English Handbook" (Draft).

Plain Language Action Network, "Plain Train–Plain Language Online Training Program." (Adapted from "Plain Language: Clear and Simple" and "Trainer's Guide to Plain Language: Clear and Simple," publications of the National Literacy Secretariat, Human Resources Development Canada.)

Plain Language Action Network, "Writing User-Friendly Documents."

Plain Language Action Network, "Simpler Words and Phrases."

Smith, Nancy M., and Ann D. Wallace, U.S. Securities and Exchange Commission, "Plain English at a Glance."

VIDEOS

Lewis, Sylvia, Director of Publications, American Planning Association, "Writing Well," American Planning Association and American Institute of Certified Planners. A classroom session with a group of planners. Covers topics such as omitting needless words, using one idea per sentence, and avoiding jargon. Includes exercises.

Glossary of Planning Acronyms

A List of Generic Terms and Organization Titles

A

AA
  Alternative Analysis
AAG
  Association of American Geographers
AASHTO
  American Association of State Highway & Transportation Officials
ACSC
  Areas of Critical State Concern
ADA
  Americans with Disabilities Act (1990)
ADT
  Average Daily Traffic (or Average Daily Trips)
ADU
  Accessory Dwelling Unit
AFT
  American Farmland Trust
AICP
  American Institute of Certified Planners
ALI
  American Law Institute
AM
  Automated Mapping

AOP

Airport Overlay District

APA

American Planning Association

APFO

Adequate Public Facilities Ordinance

APTA

American Public Transit Association

APTS

Advanced Public Transportation System

APWA

American Public Works Association

ARB

Air Resources Board

ASCE

American Society of Civil Engineers

ATC

Automated Toll Collection

ATMS

Advanced Traffic Management System

AVR

Average Vehicle Ridership

B

B-1, 2..

Business zone/use of specified intensity

BID

Business Improvement District

BLM

Bureau of Land Management (US)

BMP

Best Management Program (or Practice)

BOA

Board of Appeals or Board of Adjustment

BoCC

Board of County Commissioners

BOCA

Building Officials and Code Administrators, International

BP
   Building Permit
BTS
   Bureau of Transportation Statistics

   C
C-1, 2..
   Commercial zone/use of specified intensity
CAA
   Clean Air Act (see also FCAA)
CAD
   Computer Aided Design
CAVE
   (Pronounced Cavie) Citizens Against Virtually Everything
CBD
   Central Business District
CBDG
   Community Development Block Grant
CCD
   Census County Division
CC&R's
   Conditions, Covenants and Restrictions
CDC
   Community Development Corporation
CofA's
   Conditions of Approval
CMP
   Corrugated Metal Pipe or Construction Management Plan
CFS
   Cubic Feet per Second
CHAS
   Comprehensive Housing Affordability Strategy
CIP
   Capital Improvements Plan (or Program)
CMAQ
   Congestion Mitigation and Air Quality Program
CMSA
   Consolidated Metropolitan Statistical Area (see also MSA, SMSA, PMSA)

CO
    Certificate of Occupancy
COD
    Corridor Overlay District
COG
    Council of Governments
CRDD
    Community Residences for the Developmentally Disabled
CCRC
    Continuing Care Retirement Community
CUP
    Conditional Use Permit

D

DLG-E
    Digital Line Graph Enhanced Maps
DOE
    Department of Energy (US)
DOT
    Department of Transportation (US)
DRI
    Developments of Regional Impact
DU
    Dwelling Unit

E

EC
    Enterprise Community
ECHO
    Elder Cottage Housing Opportunities
EDA
    Economic Development Administration
EIR
    Environmental Impact Report
EIS
    Environmental Impact Statement
EMF
    Electromagnetic Field
EPA
    Environmental Protection Agency

ETC
  Employee Transportation Coordinator
EZ
  Enterprise Zone

  F
FAA
  Federal Aviation Administration
FAR
  Floor Area Ratio
FCAA
  Federal Clean Air Act
FCC
  Federal Communications Commission
FEMA
  Federal Emergency Management Agency
FGDC
  Federal Geographic Data Committee
FHA
  Federal Housing Administration
FHWA
  Federal Highway Administration
FIRE
  Finance, Insurance and Real Estate
FIA
  Fiscal Impact Analysis (also Federal Insurance
  Administration)
FM
  Facility Mapping
FMHA
  Farmers Home Administration
FNMA
  Federal National Mortgage Administration (or Fannie Mae)
FPZ
  Frontage Protection Zone
FTA
  Federal Transit Administration
  G
GDP
  General Development Plan

GFA
   Gross Floor Area
GM
   Growth Management
GIS
   Geographic Information Systems
GLA
   Gross Leasable Area
GPS
   Global Positioning System

H
HOD
   Highway Overlay District (also Historic Overlay District)
HOV
   High Occupancy Vehicle
HTF
   Housing Trust Fund
HUD
   US Department of Housing and Urban Development

I
I-1, 2..
   Industrial zone/use of specified intensity
IDA
   Industrial Development Authority
IDO
   Interim Development Ordinance
ITE
   Institute of Transportation Engineers
ICMA
   International City/County Managers Association
ISTEA
   Intermodal Surface Transportation Efficiency Act

L
LEPC
   Local Emergency Planning Committee

LBCS
  Land-Based Classification Standard
LMC
  Land Management Code
LOD
  Limits of Disturbance
LOS
  Level of Service (traffic flow rating)
LRV
  Light Rail Vehicle
LUI
  Land Use Intensity (standards developed by the Federal
  Housing Administration)
LULU
  Locally Unwanted Land Use
LUR
  Land Use Ratio

M

M-1, 2.
  Manufacturing zone/use of specified intensity
MPD
  Master Planned Community
MSA
  Metropolitan Statistical Area (see also CMSA, PMSA,
  SMSA)
MGD
  Millions of Gallons per Day
MF
  Multi-Family
MH
  Manufactured Housing
MPO
  Metropolitan Planning Organization
MTS
  Metropolitan Transportation System
MXD
  Mixed Use Development

N

NAHB
National Association of Home Builders
NAHRO
National Association of Housing & Redevelopment Officials
NAICS
North American Industrial Classification System
NARC
National Association of Regional Councils
NEPA
National Environmental Policy Act
NGO
Nongovernmental Organization
NFIP
National Flood Insurance Program
NHPA
National Historic Preservation Act
NHS
National Highway System
NIABY
Not in Anyone's Back Yard
NIMBY
Not in My Back Yard
NIMTOO
Not in My Term of Office
NRCS
National Resources Conservation Service
NRUS
Neighbors Are Us
NRI
Natural Resources Inventory
NTHP
National Trust for Historic Preservation

O

ORV
Off-Road Vehicle

P

PC
   Planning Commission
PCD
   Planned Commercial Development
PCS
   Personal Communication Services
PHT
   Peak Hour Traffic (or Peak Hour Trips)
PID
   Planned Industrial Development
PMSA
   Primary Metropolitan Statistical Area
PRD
   Planning Residential Development
PDR
   Purchase of Development Rights
PPB
   Parts Per Billion
PWS
   Public Water Supply
PPM
   Parts per Million
PUD
   Planned Unit Development
P&Z
   Planning and Zoning

Q

QOL
   Quality of Life

R

R-1,2
   Residential zone/use of specified intensity
RDA
   Redevelopment Authority

RFP
   Requests for Proposals
RFQ
   Requests for Qualifications
RFRA
   Religious Freedom Restoration Act
RPA
   Regional Planning Agency
RPC
   Regional Plan Commission
RTPA
   Regional Transportation Planning Agency
RV
   Recreational Vehicle
ROW
   Right of Way

S

SFD
   Single Family Dwelling
SAD
   Special Assessment District
SEPA
   State Environmental Protection (or Policy) Act
SCPEA
   Standard City Planning Enabling Act
SEPC
   State Emergency Planning Committee
SEQA
   State Environmental Quality Act
SF
   Single Family
SIC
   Standard Industrial Classification (Code)
SIG
   Street Index Guide
SLAPP
   Strategic Lawsuits Against Public Participation

SLO
  Sensitive Lands Ordinance
SMSA
  Standard Metropolitan Statistical Area
SOB
  Sexually Oriented Business
SOV
  Single Occupancy Vehicle
SPA
  Specifically Planned Area
SRO
  Single Room Occupancy
STP
  Surface Transportation Program
STPP
  Surface Transportation Policy Project
SZEA
  Standard (State) Zoning Enabling Act

T

TAZ
  Traffic Analysis Zone
TIF
  Tax Increment Financing
TIP
  Transportation Improvement Program
TIN
  Triangulated Irregular Network
TDM
  Transportation Demand Management
TDR
  Transfer of Development Rights
TMA
  Transportation Management Association (also
  Transportation Management Area)
TOD
  Transit Oriented Design
TRO
  Trip Reduction Ordinance

TSM
  Transportation System Management
TZO
  Temporary Zoning Ordinance

U
ULI
  Urban Land Institute
UMTA
  Urban Mass Transit Administration
URPL
  Urban and Regional Planning
USDA
  US Department of Agriculture
USDI
  US Department of the Interior
USFS
  US Forest Service
USFWS
  US Fish and Wildlife Service
USGS
  US Geological Survey
USPLS
  US Public Land Survey
UTM
  Universal Transverse Mercator Grid

V
VMT
  Vehicle Miles Traveled

W
WMD
  Watershed Management Program
WHPA
  Wellhead Protection Area
WP
  Western Planner organization and publication

WPR
   Western Planning Resources
WQMP
   Water Quality Management Plan

   X

   Y

   Z
ZBA
   Zoning Board of Adjustment (or Appeals)
ZLL
   Zero Lot Line
ZO
   Zoning Ordinance

Source: American Planning Association